CAMPUS ATTACKS
TARGETED VIOLENCE AFFECTING INSTITUTIONS OF HIGHER EDUCATION

United States Secret Service

United States Department of Education

Federal Bureau of Investigation

by

Diana A. Drysdale
Lead Social Science Research Specialist
National Threat Assessment Center
United States Secret Service

William Modzeleski
Associate Assistant Deputy Secretary
Office of Safe and Drug-Free Schools
Department of Education

Andre B. Simons
Supervisory Special Agent
Behavioral Analysis Unit
Federal Bureau of Investigation

Washington, D.C.
April 2010

U.S. Department of Homeland Security
Janet Napolitano
Secretary
U.S. Secret Service
Mark Sullivan
Director

U.S. Department of Education
Arne Duncan
Secretary
Office of Safe and Drug-Free Schools
Kevin Jennings
Assistant Deputy Secretary

U.S. Department of Justice
Eric Holder
Attorney General
Federal Bureau of Investigation
Robert S. Mueller, III
Director

April 2010

A JOINT MESSAGE FROM THE U.S. SECRET SERVICE, THE U.S. DEPARTMENT OF EDUCATION, AND THE FEDERAL BUREAU OF INVESTIGATION

In response to the Virginia Tech incident on April 16, 2007, former cabinet Secretaries Michael Leavitt and Margaret Spellings, and former Attorney General Alberto Gonzales submitted the *Report to the President on Issues Raised by the Virginia Tech Tragedy* dated June 13, 2007. The report included a recommendation that the U.S. Secret Service (Secret Service), the U.S. Department of Education, and the Federal Bureau of Investigation (FBI) explore the issue of violence at institutions of higher education (IHEs). Accordingly, we initiated a collaborative effort to understand the nature of this violence and identify ways of preventing future attacks that would affect our nation's colleges and universities.

This effort was implemented through the Secret Service's National Threat Assessment Center, the Department of Education's Office of Safe and Drug-Free Schools, and the FBI's Behavioral Analysis Unit. The project drew from the Secret Service's experience in studying threat assessment and the prevention of targeted violence; the Department of Education's expertise in helping schools facilitate learning through the creation of safe environments for students, faculty, and staff; and, the FBI's threat assessment and investigative expertise.

The goal of this collaborative endeavor was to understand the scope of the problem of targeted violence at IHEs. To that end, this report offers preliminary findings from a review of 272 incidents of violence that affected IHEs in the United States from 1900 through 2008. We addressed fundamental questions regarding where, when, and how these incidents occurred, and captured information concerning the offenders and their relationship to the IHEs. When possible, we also identified factors that may have motivated or triggered the attacks.

We strived to create a product that will be useful for threat assessment and campus safety professionals charged with identifying, assessing, and managing violence risk at IHEs. These law enforcement, mental health, student affairs, and legal professionals provide an incredible service under unique and often challenging circumstances. Ensuring the safety of college and university communities—some of which resemble small cities—is a daunting task. Navigating the intricacies of privacy laws, preserving academic freedoms, complying with civil rights laws, and simultaneously ensuring a safe campus and workplace environment are tasks not easily accomplished. We hope that this preliminary report contributes to that effort.

The Secret Service, the Department of Education, and the FBI are keenly aware of the profound and devastating physical, emotional, and psychological injuries that result from acts of violence against IHE community members and their effect on the nation as a whole. Through our collaboration, we are working to better understand what drives individuals to carry out acts of violence and ultimately how to prevent them in the future.

Paul Morrissey
Assistant Director
Office of Protective Research
United States Secret Service

William Modzeleski
Associate Assistant Deputy Secretary
Office of Safe and Drug-Free Schools
Department of Education

Robert A. Blecksmith
Assistant Director
Critical Incident Response Group
Federal Bureau of Investigation

Acknowledgements

The authors would like to thank project staff from each of the participating agencies for their invaluable contributions. At the U.S. Secret Service's National Threat Assessment Center (NTAC), these individuals include: Michelle Keeney, J.D., Ph.D., Lina Alathari, Ph.D., Eileen Kowalski, Tracey Mullins, Sergeant Rolanda Brodie, and Sergeant Timothy Burns. For the U.S. Department of Education's Office of Safe and Drug-Free Schools, these individuals include: Elizabeth Argeris, Deborah Rudy, and Tara Hill. The authors would also like to thank Kari DeCelle of the U.S. Department of Education's Readiness and Emergency Management for Schools Technical Assistance Center (REMS TA) for designing the cover. The Federal Bureau of Investigation's Behavioral Analysis Unit (BAU) would like to thank: Supervisory Special Agent (SSA) Shawn F. VanSlyke, Yvonne E. Muirhead, Katherine A. Schoeneman, Ph.D.,Erin K. Nekvasil, and SSA David T. Resch. The BAU extends its gratitude to: Lesley A. Buckles, Helene V. Christensen, Allison Grupski, Meghann Hudson, Leigh Ann Perry, Kari L. Riddles, Kimberly C. Stamatopoulos, Elizabeth Sutton, and Maria Valdovinos.

This project also benefited from the thoughtful comments of a subject matter expert group comprising representatives from campus law enforcement, threat assessment professionals, and higher education. Participants included: Eugene Deisinger, Ph.D., Christopher Flynn, Ph.D., Steven J. Healy, Gary Lyle, Kris Mohandie, Ph.D., Mario J. Scalora, Ph.D., and Vasti Torres, Ph.D.

INTRODUCTION

On April 16, 2007, Seung Hui Cho, 23, a student at Virginia Polytechnic Institute and State University ("Virginia Tech") in Blacksburg, Virginia, carried out what would become one of the deadliest school shootings in the world. Around 7:15 a.m., Cho fatally shot a female student in her dormitory room in West Ambler Johnston Residential Hall and then shot the building's residential advisor. Approximately two-and-a-half hours later, Cho entered Norris Hall, a lecture building, and shot numerous students and faculty before killing himself. In total, Cho killed 32 (27 students and five faculty members) and wounded 17. Some of the wounded individuals were struck by gunfire while others were injured trying to jump from the building.

This killing spree stunned the nation and questions echoed throughout the country from parents, administrators, and government officials alike. In response, Virginia Governor Timothy Kaine established the Virginia Tech Review Panel (VTRP) on June 18, 2007, to gain a better understanding of the incident and its underlying causes so that steps could be taken to minimize the chances of a similar tragedy happening again.[1]

At the federal level, President George W. Bush charged Attorney General Alberto Gonzales, Department of Education Secretary Margaret Spellings, and Department of Health and Human Services Secretary Michael Leavitt to convene meetings throughout the country focused on the issues raised by the Virginia Tech tragedy. Meetings were subsequently held with college and university representatives, local and state leaders, law enforcement officials, and mental health care providers. President Bush instructed Secretary Leavitt to summarize the lessons learned from these meetings and to recommend how the federal government could help prevent similar incidents in the future.

On June 13, 2007, based upon the meeting discussions as well as other input, the *Report to the President on Issues Raised by the Virginia Tech Tragedy* was issued.[2] This report presented a series of findings, common themes, observations, and recommendations, one of which stated: "The U.S. Department of Education, in collaboration with the U.S. Secret Service and the Department of Justice, should explore research of targeted violence in institutions of higher education and continue to share existing threat assessment methodology with interested institutions."[3,4] To that end, representatives from the U.S. Secret Service (Secret Service), the U.S. Department of Education, and the Federal Bureau of Investigation (FBI) initiated a partnership in pursuit of this goal.

The three entities began by asking fundamental questions, such as: How prevalent are the incidents of targeted violence that affect institutions of higher education (IHEs)? Who are the

---

[1] Virginia Tech Review Panel. (2007, August). *Mass shootings at Virginia Tech, April 16, 2007: Report of the Review Panel.* Retrieved July 8, 2008, from www.vtreviewpanel.org/report/index.html.

[2] U.S. Department of Health and Human Services. (2007, June 13). *Report to the President on issues raised by the Virginia Tech tragedy.* Retrieved August 21, 2008, from http://www.hhs.gov/vtreport.html#intro. Hereafter referred to as the "Report to the President."

[3] "Targeted violence" is defined as an incident of violence where a known or knowable attacker selects a particular target prior to their violent attack. See Fein, R.A., Vossekuil, B., & Holden, G. (1995, September). Threat assessment: An approach to prevent targeted violence. *Research in Action (NCJ 155000).* Washington, D.C.: U.S. Department of Justice, Office of Justice Programs, National Institute of Justice.

[4] *Report to the President*, p. 9.

perpetrators? Are they affiliated with the affected IHE? There was limited previous research on these issues, so the initial framework for the project became clear to the three agencies, which began a comprehensive effort to identify, through open-sources, incidents of targeted violence that have affected IHE communities.

This report provides an overview of these incidents and the involved subjects, discusses initial observations regarding behaviors of the subjects, and offers preliminary considerations regarding the data that may have relevance to threat assessment. While the participating agencies are aware of the limitations of an open-source descriptive review, this preliminary effort will be complemented by a more in-depth study to be conducted by the Department of Education and the FBI.

BACKGROUND

The specific phenomenon of targeted violence at institutions of higher education (IHEs) should be considered within its own context. This section begins by reviewing the previous incident-based research, defining the IHE community, and discussing what forms of criminal activity exist within this community.

Previous Incident-Based Research

To better understand the breadth of issues with which an IHE may be confronted as part of a threat assessment, the Secret Service, Department of Education, and the FBI sought to identify and review literature that specifically examined the full-range of incidents of targeted violence affecting IHEs.

As noted by former Secretary Spellings, along with former Attorney General Gonzales and former Secretary Leavitt, a number of law enforcement officers, mental health care providers, school officials, and educators have cited the publication, *Threat Assessment in Schools: A Guide to Managing Threatening Situations and to Creating Safe School Climates.*[5] This guide was published jointly by the Secret Service and the Department of Education in May 2002. It was based upon the Safe School Initiative (SSI), a research project that examined 37 incidents of targeted school shootings that occurred between 1974 and 2000 at elementary, middle, and high schools. This landmark study identified observable pre-attack behaviors of student perpetrators in K-12 schools and highlighted several strategies for recognizing and managing persons who pose a threat to school populations.

When considering whether these findings are applicable to similar incidents within an IHE setting, it is important to note that specific and observable pre-attack behaviors demonstrated by attackers at the college or university level have yet to be thoroughly examined for comparison. Applying the findings of the SSI to IHE-based populations may provide appropriate prompts and insights to guide threat assessment, but there are important differences that may impact the threat assessment process.

At a basic level, the physical environment of a K-12 setting is vastly different from that of a college or university setting. Secondary schools typically comprise one to several buildings, utilize smaller classrooms, and provide an experience in which students have regular contact with the same faculty and staff. Communication between responsible parties regarding issues facing the student population is facilitated by this proximity. For the most part, numerous educators are aware of students' whereabouts and behaviors during each school day. Additionally, faculty meetings enable information sharing and increase the likelihood of recognizing behaviors of concern. In contrast, IHE campuses usually comprise many buildings, often with larger classrooms, separate faculty for each department, more uncontrolled access and egress, and irregular student schedules that minimize regular contact between educators and

---

[5] Fein, R., Vossekuil, B., Borum, R., Pollack, W. S., Modzeleski, W., and Reddy, M. (2002, May). *Threat assessment in schools: A guide to managing threatening situations and to creating safe school climates.* Washington, DC: United States Secret Service and United States Department of Education.

students. These factors are less conducive to observing and recognizing behavioral concerns among the student population.

At a more nuanced level, the developmental and social differences between high school students and college students suggest that IHE-based subjects may engage in pre-attack behaviors that differ from those of their high school counterparts. A college or university campus may be both an educational and a residential environment, making it a setting in which significant developmental and transitional stressors are ushered into a person's life. This combination is not often found in other settings. For the student who has just moved away from home, there are numerous environmental changes that can introduce a new dimension of stress. Some challenges include establishing self-sufficiency and responsibility, academic pressures, social pressures, and personal health and safety decisions. The student's coping skills can range from positive, such as seeking counseling or talking with friends, to negative, such as social withdrawal and isolation or alcohol and drug abuse.

When behaviors of concern are identified among secondary school students, there exists the potential for educators and threat assessment personnel to communicate with parents to solicit family involvement. However, options for the IHE official are more limited, as regular communication with parents is less likely to occur for a variety of reasons and IHE students who live away from home must reach out for services independently.

Beyond the SSI, there is limited research on IHE-related targeted violence that contains comprehensive incident analysis. The majority of the literature offers practical guidance on conducting threat assessments, preventing targeted violence, and handling the aftermath of an incident. There is some research on handfuls of incidents across all educational levels, not just IHEs, and in-depth case analyses focused on only a few incidents. The research has also addressed particular aspects of violence on IHE campuses, such as stalking, domestic violence, courtship violence, campus sexual assault, hazing, and drug/alcohol induced violence. Various surveys have been published that attempt to assess the frequency of violent crime affecting IHE communities. However, these surveys collected limited information and were focused on specific campuses, geographical areas, and timeframes. The relevance of this information is not in question, but the existing literature has generally looked at these issues in isolation and does not allow us to look across types of violence to gauge the relative prevalence and context.

One of the few reports to look across the spectrum was Max L. Bromley's *Campus-Related Murders: A Content Analysis Review of News Articles.*[6] Bromley examined *Chronicle of Higher Education* articles from 1989 to 2001 for incidents of campus murder to gain a deeper understanding of the offenders, victims, circumstances, and university or college response. Analysis of 33 incidents highlighted the fact that college campuses share commonalities with the communities at large with regard to murders. As in the general population, Bromley found, examples of domestic, intimate, and workplace violence were present in campus homicide cases. In a majority of the studied cases, there was some kind of relationship between the offender and the victim, and both tended to be members of the campus community (students, faculty, or staff).

---

[6] Bromley, M. L. (2005). *Campus-related murders: A content analysis review of news articles.* Paper presented at the Annual Conference of the Southern Criminal Justice Association. Retrieved September 25, 2008, from http://www.dcf.state.fl.us Updated link retrieved on April 14, 2010: http://www.dcf.state.fl.us/initiatives/campussecurity/docs/Campus_Related_Murders050907.pdf.

Handguns and other weapons were used in about half of the campus murders, which mirrored the rate of murders involving handguns in the general community. Bromley noted that, despite these shared features, "little is known at this time about the nature and characteristics of murders on campus."

As the professional literature does not offer a comprehensive perspective that examines the full-range of incidents faced by IHEs, the search focused on published lists of incidents of school-related violence. These lists typically reflected the following limitations: (1) the manner in which they were compiled was not always documented; (2) they lacked stated and clearly defined criteria for the inclusion of incidents; (3) they blended incidents from all educational levels (i.e., elementary, secondary, and postsecondary); (4) they often combined incidents that occurred within the United States and those that occurred on foreign soil; (5) they frequently focused on the more well-known incidents; and (6) they presented only basic information about each incident, such as the date, location, name of the subjects and/or victims, and a brief description of what occurred.

A review of the existing literature and resources confirmed the need for the Secret Service, the Department of Education, and the FBI to compile a comprehensive inventory of targeted violence incidents that have affected IHE communities.

Defining the IHE Community

According to the *Digest of Education Statistics: 2008 (The Digest)*,[7] there were 6,563 postsecondary Title IV Institutions in 2006-07.[8] Of these institutions, 4,314 were degree-granting[9] and 2,222 were non-degree-granting.[10]

Focusing primarily on the 4,314 degree-granting institutions, 2,629 (approximately 60 percent) were four-year colleges or universities, and 1,685 (approximately 40 percent) were two-year colleges. Student enrollment in these institutions in the fall of 2006 measured 17.8 million (11.2 million in four-year institutions and 6.5 million in two-year institutions).[11, 12] Of these students,

---

[7] Snyder, T.D., Dillow, S.A., and Hoffman, C.M. (2009, March). *Digest of Education Statistics 2008 (NCES 2009-020)*. Washington, DC: National Center for Education Statistics, Institute of Education Sciences, U.S. Department of Education. Retrieved June 1, 2009, from http://nces.ed.gov. Hereafter referred to as "The Digest."

[8] Title IV institutions are defined as "all post-secondary institutions whose students are eligible to participate in the Title IV federal financial aid programs." Table 5. Number of educational institutions, by level and control of institution: Selected years, 1980–81 through 2006–07, *The Digest*, p. 19.

[9] Degree-granting institutions are defined as "postsecondary institutions that grant an associate's or higher degree and whose students are eligible to participate in the Title IV federal financial aid programs. Degree-granting institutions include almost all 2- and 4-year colleges and universities; they exclude institutions offering only vocational programs of less than 2 years duration and continuing education programs." *The Digest*, p. 269.

[10] Non-degree granting included institutions that "did not offer accredited 4-year or 2-year degree programs, but were participating in Title IV federal financial aid programs. Includes some schools with non-accredited degree programs." *The Digest*, p. 269.

[11] Table 186. Enrollment, staff, and degrees conferred in postsecondary institutions participating in Title IV programs, by type and control of institution, sex of student, type of staff, and type of degree: fall 2005, fall 2006, and 2006–07. *The Digest*, p. 276.

[12] These numbers may not equal the 17.8 million shown due to rounding. Not included in these numbers were an additional 446,604 students enrolled in non-degree-granting institutions.

42.7 percent were male and 57.3 percent were female. The youngest enrolled students were reported to be age 14; however, ages beyond 35 were not specified (see Table 1).[13]

The majority of the enrolled students in the fall of 2006 attended larger colleges and universities. Specifically, campuses boasting enrollment levels of 10,000 students or more represented only 12 percent of the institutions; however, they enrolled 55 percent of all college students.[14] By comparison, 41 percent of the institutions had enrollment levels of less than 1,000 students, and these institutions enrolled only 4 percent of all college students.

Table 1: Student Enrollment, by Age Group, Fall 2006

Age	Enrollment	%
14-17	231,000	1.3
18-19	3,769,000	21.2
20-21	3,648,000	20.5
22-24	3,193,000	18.0
25-29	2,401,000	13.5
30-34	1,409,000	7.9
Over 35	3,107,000	17.5
Total	17,758,000	100

In addition to students, IHE communities comprise employees that include faculty, administration, and support staff. In the fall of 2007, 3.6 million people were employed at degree-granting institutions.[15] This number includes 2.6 million professional staff (including faculty, executive/administrative/ managerial personnel, graduate assistants, and other professionals) and 932,027 non-professional staff (including technical/clerical/secretarial personnel, skilled trade persons, and maintenance staff). Sixty-four percent of the employees worked on a full-time basis, while the remaining 36 percent were part-time. Overall, the employee population was 46 percent male and 54 percent female.[16] Age distributions were not reported.

IHE Campus Crime

Maintaining the safety of IHEs and the students and employees that comprise IHE communities is a vital task. The statistics reported as part of the *Crime Awareness and Campus Security Act of 1990* offer a gauge of the level and type of crime that takes place on college campuses. Amended three times in 1992, 1998, and 2000, this act was renamed in 1998 the *Jeanne Clery Disclosure of Campus Security Policy and Campus Crime Statistics Act*, or the *Clery Act*, in memory of a student who was killed in her dormitory room in 1986. In response to the Virginia Tech shootings, Congress further amended the act in 2008, adding a campus emergency response plan to its requirements. The amendment requires IHEs to "immediately notify" the campus community as soon as an emergency is confirmed on the campus unless such notification would impede attempts to control the situation.

The *Clery Act* requires all colleges and universities that participate in the federal financial aid programs under Title IV of the *Higher Education Act* to maintain and disclose information about certain crimes committed on or near campuses. The *Clery Act* defines these crimes as they are defined in the FBI's Uniform Crime Reporting Handbook (UCR).

Specifically, campus personnel must track and report criminal homicides, including murder, negligent and non-negligent manslaughter, sex offenses (including forcible and non-forcible),

---

[13] Table 190. Total fall enrollment in degree-granting institutions, by sex, age, and attendance status: Selected years, 1970 through 2017. *The Digest*, p. 280.

[14] *The Digest*, p. 270.

[15] Statistics were reported for fall 2005 and fall 2007 only.

[16] Table 243. Employees in degree-granting institutions, by sex, employment status, control and type of institution, and primary occupation: Selected years, fall 1987 through fall 2007. *The Digest*, p. 358.

robbery, aggravated assault, burglary, motor vehicle theft, and arson. They must also report whether any of these crimes, other crimes involving bodily harm, or larceny, theft, simple assault, intimidation, and destruction, damage or vandalism of property were hate crimes. Statistics are also required for arrests and disciplinary action referrals for weapons possession or drug and alcohol law violations.

Under the *Clery Act*, criminal activity must also be broken down by location, whether "on campus, in or on a non-campus building or property, or on public property within or immediately adjacent to and accessible from the campus."[17] Finally, the *Clery Act* does not make any distinction regarding the resolution of the reported crimes (unless deemed to be unfounded by law enforcement) and does not limit the reported crimes to those that affected or were committed by IHE students or employees.

Table 2 depicts the number of crimes reported to the Department of Education in compliance with the *Clery Act* from 2005 through 2008.[18] Data were reported by public and private institutions ranging from four-year and above to less than two-year. Those institutions with multiple campuses reported data for each campus. Looking at all 235,599 crimes reported over this timeframe, 74.6 percent were burglaries and motor vehicle thefts, 9.2 percent were aggravated assaults, 8.4 percent were robberies, 5.9 percent were forcible sex offenses, 1.7 percent were arsons, and 0.1 percent were non-forcible sex offenses. The remaining 0.1 percent of reported crimes were murders and non-negligent manslaughter (0.07 percent, $n = 174$) and negligent manslaughter (0.02 percent, $n = 46$).[19] Of the 174 murders and non-negligent manslaughters, 80 occurred on campus (13 of which took place in residence halls), 82 occurred on public property immediately adjacent to campuses, and 12 occurred at non-campus facilities.

Table 2: Crime Statistics Reported in Compliance with the *Clery Act*, by Type of Crime and Year: 2005-08

	Murder / Non-Negligent Manslaughter	Negligent Manslaughter	Forcible Sex Offense	Non-Forcible Sex Offense	Robbery	Aggravated Assault	Burglary	Motor Vehicle Theft	Arson
2005	28	33	3,583	55	5,432	5,943	37,800	11,890	1,219
2006	25	0	3,490	56	4,921	5,472	35,124	9,811	1,086
2007	66	8	3,482	62	4,985	5,234	33,010	8,744	915
2008	55	5	3,287	49	4,562	5,026	31,851	7,465	825
Total	174	46	13,842	222	19,900	21,675	137,785	37,910	4,045

Although murder and non-negligent homicide represent the second smallest percentage of crimes reported by campus officials, the prevention of these types of crimes is a priority among IHE officials. The current effort between the Secret Service, the Department of Education, and the FBI seeks to identify for study a subset of these crimes—that is, incidents of targeted violence—to support prevention efforts.

---

[17] U.S. Department of Education, Office of Postsecondary Education. (2005, June). The handbook for campus crime reporting, p. 11. Retrieved September 25, 2008, from http://www.ed.gov/admins/lead/safety/handbook.pdf. Also see Higher Education Act, 34 C.F.R. 668.46(a) for full definitions of campus, and public property.

[18] U.S. Department of Education, Office of Postsecondary Education. (n.d.) The campus security data analysis cutting tool, aggregated data for calendar years 2005-07 and 2006-2008 [spreadsheets]. Retrieved July 22, 2009, from http://ope.ed.gov/security/. Numbers shown for 2005 were taken from the aggregate data for 2005-07. Numbers shown for 2006-08 were taken from the aggregate data for 2006-08.

[19] These numbers may not equal the 0.1 percent shown due to rounding.

DEFINING AND IDENTIFYING THE INCIDENTS

The partner agencies designed and launched an effort to identify a broad range of incidents that have affected IHEs. The goal of this effort was to identify relevant incidents involving directed assaults and to gather information on the key incident elements that could be gleaned from open-source reporting. To ensure that the scope encompassed the many issues that an IHE may face, incidents affecting postsecondary vocational and proprietary schools were also included.[20]

Inclusion Criteria

Criteria were determined in advance to guide the selection of incidents for inclusion. As the term "targeted violence" lacks the degree of specificity necessary for incident criteria, for the purposes of this report, we have selected and defined a more precise term that will reflect the full spectrum of incidents. Relevant incidents were defined as **directed assaults** in which open-source reporting suggested they met the following four criteria:

    (a) The Target(s):
        (1) The subject(s) selected a *specific* IHE Student(s), IHE Employee(s), or IHE Facility/Event(s) as a target (see Appendix A for definitions), or
        (2) The subject(s) selected a *random* IHE Student(s), IHE Employee(s), or IHE Facility/Event(s) because the target's characteristics matched the subject's victim profile.[21]

    (b) Timing of Target Selection:
        (1) The target(s) was selected *prior to the initiation of the assault*, or
        (2) The target(s) was selected *at the time of the assault* based on a victim profile or the subject's personal pre-existing relationship with the target(s) (e.g., roommates, friends, romantics).

    (c) Lethality of Assault: The subject(s) *employed or had the present ability to employ lethal force*.[22]

    (d) Timeframe and Geographical Limitations:
        (1) The incident occurred between *January 1, 1900*[23] *and December 31, 2008*,
        (2) The incident occurred **on-campus, off-campus**, or in/around a **non-campus** facility (see additional criteria below; see Appendix A for definitions), and
        (3) The incident occurred *within the United States.*

---

[20] The question of whether the affected IHEs were Title IV institutions or degree-granting was set aside for case identification purposes as the Title IV designation was not in effect until after the passage of *The Higher Education Act of 1965* and the accreditation status of particular schools evolved over time.

[21] "Victim profile" is defined as a set of demographic or other perceived static traits that the subject(s) sought in selecting a target(s). Example: A subject goes to an IHE campus looking for a blond college-aged female to abduct and kill as part of a fantasy.

[22] "Lethal" is defined as causing or capable of causing death. Crimes of a sexual nature were included only if the subject actually employed lethal physical force.

[23] Due to the limited availability of searchable media reporting prior to 1900, this year was selected as the start date.

For incidents that took place off-campus and involved two persons in a romantic, spousal, or co-habitant/roommate relationship, both the subject and the target must have been affiliated with the affected IHE, with at least one of their affiliations current.

In general, incidents that fell within any of the following areas were excluded: hazing, pranks, crimes primarily motivated by material gain, murder-for-hire schemes connected to a separate crime, incidents perpetrated by ideological groups or arising from general social disorder, low-level assaults on facilities with little to no capacity to cause injuries or fatalities, gang and drug-related violence, spontaneous altercations between strangers, and incidents with insufficient information to determine whether they met the inclusion criteria. These latter incidents included those in which either the subject was not identified in open-source reports or the case remained unsolved at the time the research was performed. Additionally, incidents involving serial killers who were not formerly or currently affiliated with the affected IHE were also excluded.

Methodology and Limitations

Incidents were identified from open-source reporting via a three-step process. First, lists of school-related incidents of violence available on the Internet and published documents were reviewed. Thirty-one incidents from these previously compiled lists and publications met the definition of a directed assault. Second, a complex search string was developed and applied to the Nexis "All English News Group." Language used to describe the incidents identified in the first step served as the basis for the construction of this search string. Although news articles from 1970 through 2008 were reviewed, it is important to note that the media coverage contained in Nexis is sparse until the 1990s. After reviewing over 111,800 search results, an additional 198 incidents were identified that met the definition of a directed assault. Finally, a phrase-based search was executed in NewspaperArchive.com on available articles from 1759 through 1990. After screening over 3,600 search results, 43 additional incidents were identified that met criteria for inclusion. At the completion of this effort, it was determined that only those cases that took place from 1900 onward would be included due to the limitations of the press coverage prior to that year. The final sample consists of 272 incidents identified through this search process.

Data gathered for each incident included specific case information and qualitative observations. The specific case information fell within the categories of incident overview (e.g., date, location, type of IHE), incident specifics (e.g., site of attack, weapon used), subject descriptors (e.g., affiliation with IHE, gender, age), and incident outcome (e.g., injuries, deaths, judicial status). Data underwent a four-stage review process by a minimum of three researchers to verify the information gathered. Variables were created to capture the qualitative observations, which characterized the subject's apparent motives and triggers, targeting, and pre-incident behaviors. Two researchers independently coded these variables following a prescribed protocol. When necessary, additional research was performed to fill in gaps or clarify points using the three resources named above, Lexis-Nexis federal and state case law databases, and open Internet searches.

As all information obtained about the incidents was limited to open-source materials, it is important to emphasize a few of the limitations inherent in using such data for behavioral research. First, since this sample only includes those incidents that were reported in the media, it is possible that there were other directed assaults at IHEs that met the inclusion criteria during the same timeframe. Second, as the level of detail reported varied significantly across incidents, data collected was limited to what could reasonably be collected for each case. Finally, we recognize that media reporting often contains objective and subjective errors. While the former are factual or mechanical in nature, the latter involve errors in the meaning or interpretation of the events.[24] When challenged with conflicting reports across sources, consideration was given to a number of factors, including the apparent quality of reporting, timing of the reporting, location of the media outlet in relation to the incident, and the source cited in the report. No efforts were made to check the veracity of reporting against primary sources other than when legal documents were available in Lexis. Given these limitations, the reader is reminded that this undertaking is purely descriptive, and is not comparative or predictive.

---

[24] Singletary, M. (1980, January 25). *Accuracy in the news reporting: A review of the research (No. 25)*. Washington, DC: ANPA News Research Center. Retrieved on January 8, 2010, from http://www.eric.ed.gov/ERICDocs/data/ ericdocs2sql/content_storage_01/0000019b/80/32/9e/5b.pdf; and, Maier, S. (2002). Getting it Right? Not in 59 Percent of Stories. *Newspaper Research Journal*, 23 (1). Retrieved on January 8, 2010, from http://www.questia.com.

THE FINDINGS

Although the following results should be viewed in light of the limitations related to open-source reporting, this information does offer perspectives on the breadth and key aspects of the 272 incidents of targeted violence that serve as the basis for this report.

Where in the United States did the incidents occur?

Incidents were identified in 42 states and the District of Columbia, with 57 percent ($n = 155$) of the incidents affecting IHEs located in only 10 states,[25] eight of which are among the 10 states with the most IHEs.[26] The majority of the incidents affected IHEs designated as 4-year institutions (84 percent, $n = 228$), followed by 2-year institutions (14 percent, $n = 38$), postsecondary vocational/technical schools (1 percent, $n = 4$), and those institutions identified as post-graduate only (1 percent, $n = 2$).[27] In all, incidents affected 218 distinct campuses.

When did the incidents occur?

Targeted violence affecting IHEs is not a new phenomenon (see Table 3). The first incident identified that met criteria occurred on April 29, 1909. On this date, a subject, who was not affiliated with the affected IHE, fatally shot his former girlfriend, a student, on her college campus. He then killed himself. The target had reportedly refused the subject's marriage proposals. He had come to the college two to three days earlier to persuade the target to change her mind.

The majority of incidents occurred during the 1990s and 2000s. It is unknown what may have caused the increase in incidents identified during the past 20 years. However, consideration should be given to the increased enrollment levels at IHEs as well as the increase in media coverage and digital reporting throughout the United States over the past few decades.

Figure 1 shows the increase in fall student enrollment levels at postsecondary, degree-granting institutions from 1909 through 2009 (projected).[28] It also shows the number of incidents identified by decade from the 1900s through the 2000s. Generally, as enrollment levels increased over time, so did the number of reported incidents.

Table 3: Directed Assaults by Decade, 1900-2008

Decade	$N =$	%
1900s	1	0.4
1910s	0	0.0
1920s	3	1.1
1930s	8	2.9
1940s	1	0.4
1950s	13	4.8
1960s	19	7.0
1970s	25	9.2
1980s	40	14.7
1990s	79	29.0
2000s*	83	30.5
Total	272	100.0

* Data collected through 2008.

---

[25] From highest to lowest number of incidents, these 10 states are: California, New York, Texas, Florida, Michigan, Ohio, Pennsylvania, Illinois, Indiana, and North Carolina.

[26] Table 266: Degree-granting institutions and branches, by type and control of institution and state or jurisdiction: 2007–08. Of note, looking at the media sources searched in Lexis-Nexis, the largest resource used in identifying incidents, the states with the most incidents coincided with the states with the most newspapers and wire services.

[27] Percentages may add up to more than 100 percent due to rounding.

[28] Table 3. Enrollment in educational institutions, by level and control of institution: Selected years, 1869-70. *The Digest,* p. 16.

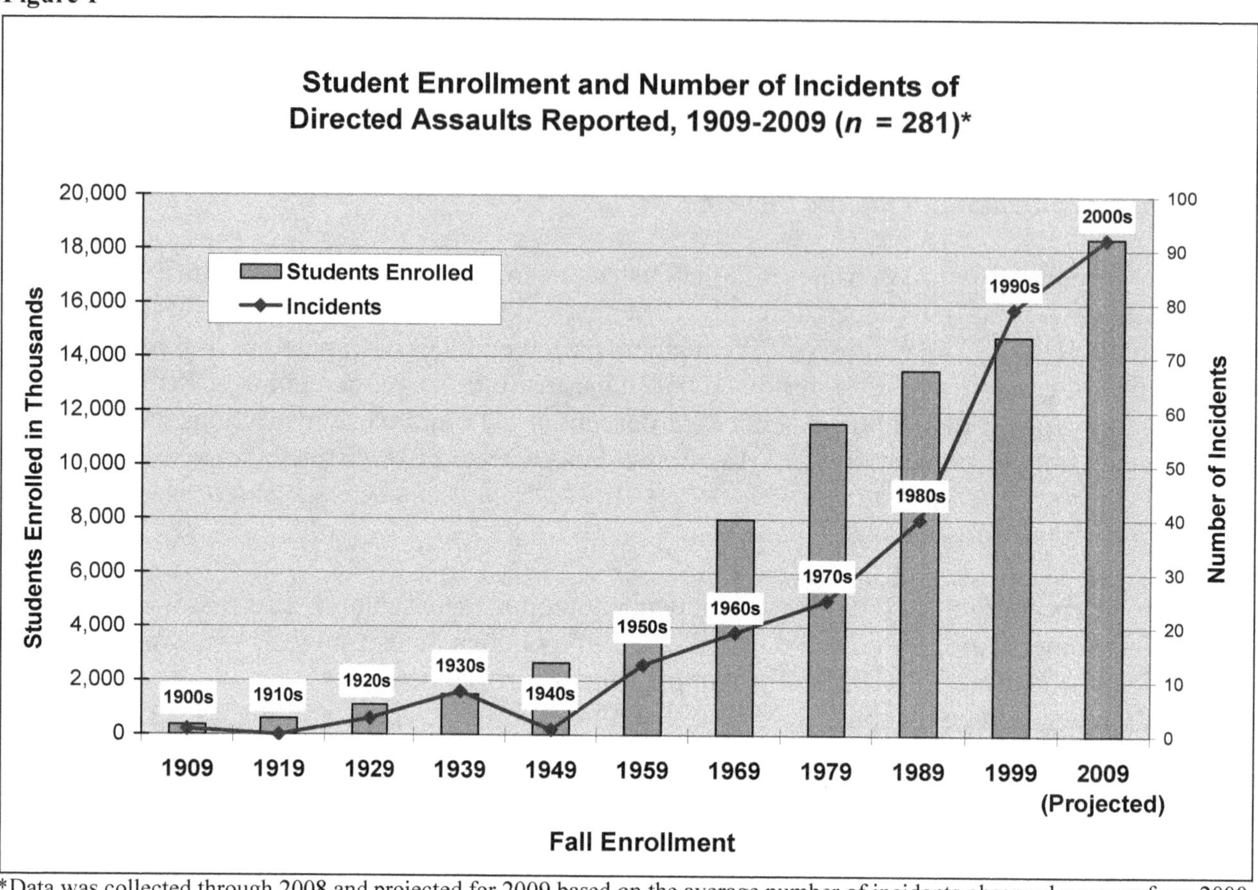

*Data was collected through 2008 and projected for 2009 based on the average number of incidents observed per year from 2000 to 2008. Pearson (r = 0.924, p< 0.000) correlation is significant at the 0.01 level (1-tailed).

Incidents also occurred throughout the calendar year ($n = 270$).[29] Figure 2 shows that although there was a decrease in the frequency, incidents happened even during the summer months.

Figure 2

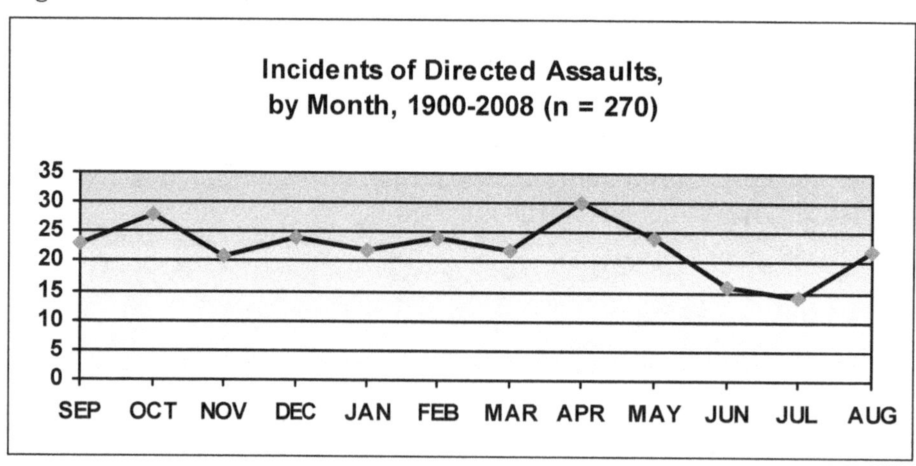

[29] For two of the incidents, the months in which they occurred could not be determined from open-source reporting.

Where did the incidents occur in relation to the IHE?

It may initially seem as though only incidents occurring on-campus are relevant to understanding targeted violence that affects IHEs. However, such a view neglects the role of campus safety departments and campus threat assessment teams in securing the area surrounding the campus and assessing the threats posed by and to IHE students, faculty, and staff, regardless of whether the ultimate act of violence occurs within the confines of the campus boundaries. Thus, the current project aimed to identify incidents that could fall within the purview of a campus threat assessment. A majority of the incidents occurred on-campus (79percent, $n = 214$), while approximately one-fifth (19 percent, $n = 52$) were off-campus. The remaining six incidents occurred either at non-campus[30] locations (1 percent, $n = 3$) or at undetermined sites (1 percent, $n = 3$).

Of those incidents that occurred at on-campus or non-campus sites ($n = 217$), similar numbers of incidents took place in residential buildings (28 percent, $n = 60$), parking lots or campus grounds (27 percent, $n = 58$), and administrative and/or academic buildings such as offices, classrooms, laboratories (26 percent, $n = 56$; see Table 4). In only 3 percent ($n = 6$) of the on/non-campus incidents did the subject move from the campus grounds or parking lots to buildings, move between buildings, or cause injuries and/or deaths in more than one location on campus. In addition to the Virginia Tech attack in 2007, two other examples in which subjects moved from one location or building to another are the following:

Table 4: On and Non-campus Directed Assaults, by Building, 1900-2008

Buildings	$n =$	%
IHE Residence	60	27.7
IHE Grounds & Parking Lots	58	26.7
Administrative or Academic	56	25.8
Student/Employee Services	22	10.1
Other/Undetermined	15	6.9
Multiple Facilities/Buildings	6	2.8
Total	217	100.0

On August 1, 1966, a 25-year-old student and former marine seized an observation tower on campus, killing and/or injuring several people on his way up the tower, then randomly fired a rifle at passersby for approximately 96 minutes. He was eventually shot by police. In the aftermath, 13 people were killed and 31 were wounded on the campus. The evening before the incident, the subject typed a final letter of explanation detailing his thoughts. He then went to his mother's home, choking and fatally stabbing her shortly after midnight. After writing another letter, which he left there, he returned home and fatally stabbed his wife as she slept. Penning notes to other family members, he prepared for his attack later that day.

On December 14, 1992, an 18-year-old student killed one professor, one student, and wounded four others in a random sweep across campus. The subject first approached a security-guard shack on the campus and shot the guard inside. Critically wounding him, he then fatally shot a professor, who was driving past. From there, he walked to the library where he fatally shot a student. He then entered a dormitory and resumed firing. He surrendered to police after his rifle jammed and he called 911, informing them that he was the shooter. Reportedly, the subject held views that were perceived as racist, homophobic and anti-Semitic by fellow students and was not adjusting well to the campus environment.

See Appendix B for descriptions of the remaining three incidents.

---

[30] See Appendix A for definition.

Of the incidents that occurred within an IHE owned/operated building ($n = 159$), over half of them took place in dorm rooms or apartments, offices, and instructional areas such as classrooms, lecture halls, or laboratories ($n = 90$, 57 percent; see Table 5).

Table 5: Directed Assaults within IHE Buildings, by Locale, 1900-2008

Locales	$n =$	%
Dorm Room or Apartment	48	30.2
Office(s)	22	13.8
Instructional Area	20	12.6
Non-specific/Other/Undetermined	16	10.1
Common Area	15	9.4
Hallway(s)/Stairwell(s)/Restroom(s)	15	9.4
Student Services Locales/Cafeteria	10	6.3
Multiple Locales within the Same Building	7	4.4
Multiple Facilities/Buildings	6	3.8
Total	159	100

Several subjects also carried out their attacks in multiple locales within the same building, moving from offices and classrooms to common areas, causing injuries and deaths at the different locales (4 percent, $n = 7$). One example includes the following:

On October 28, 2002, a 41-year-old student entered a college building shortly before 8:30 a.m., looking for three instructors. The subject fatally shot the first in her 2nd-floor office. He then fatally shot the second in a 4th-floor classroom in front of approximately 20 students, walked to the back of the classroom and shot his final victim. Soon after, he released the students and shot himself. The subject had been failing and had mailed a 22-page letter and other documents to a local media outlet. In his letter, he sketched his failed marriage, poor health, and the slights he perceived from the nursing school he claimed treated male students as "tokens."

See Appendix B for descriptions of remaining six incidents.

In turning to those incidents that occurred off-campus ($n = 52$), most took place at a private residence (75 percent, $n = 39$), while approximately one-fifth of the incidents occurred outside of a structure (e.g., on a sidewalk, in a parking lot; 19 percent, $n = 10$). Two examples of incidents that occurred off-campus include the following:

On December 11, 1949, a 24-year-old student strangled his girlfriend, a fellow student, after a fraternity party at an off-campus men's rooming house. Two months prior, a university psychiatrist had treated the subject for suicidal ideations and an impulse to kill said girlfriend.

On February 16, 2004, a 38-year-old former student who had worked for a psychology professor at a test center stalked her, went to her off-campus private residence, stabbed, and decapitated her. He then stripped off his clothing and ran in front of a truck on the highway, killing himself.

Who were the subjects?

Efforts were made to gather information regarding the subjects who carried out the attacks. The majority of incidents were perpetrated by one individual ($n = 270$) and, of those, most of the subjects were male (94 percent, $n = 254$).[31] In the incidents where age was reported ($n = 260$), the range was 16 to 62, with an average age of 28 (*Mdn* = 25, mode = 20). See Figure 3 for a depiction of the number of incidents by subject age groups.

Figure 3

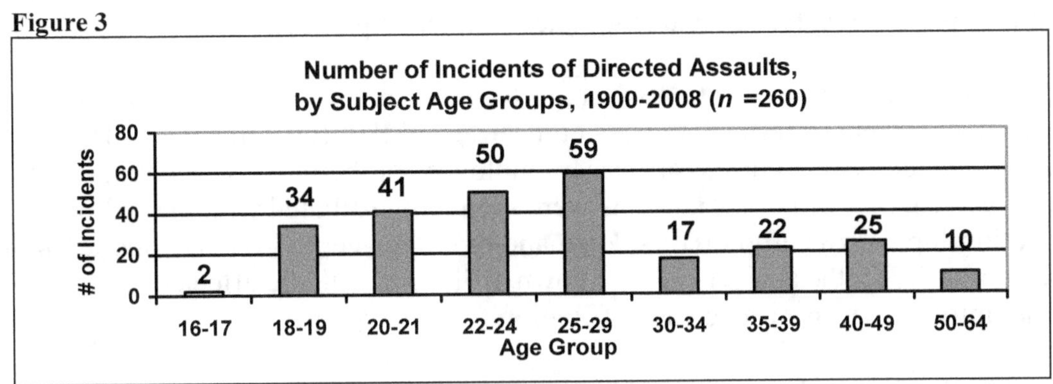

The Youngest Subject:

On October 10, 1993, a 16-year-old male who was not affiliated with the affected IHE, detonated a pipe bomb outside the dorm room of two black students. Though no injuries were reported, the building was "severely damaged" by the racially motivated attack. The subject, who had tried to join a white supremacist organization, had admitted responsibility to witnesses and vowed to shoot all the black students at the college.

One of the Two Oldest Subjects:

On October 13, 2008, a 62-year-old, part-time librarian fatally shot a fellow full-time librarian, allegedly after a dispute the previous night over "work ethics." After the shooting, the subject sat down and calmly waited for police.

Of note, among the cases there were three subjects who carried out multiple attacks on the same campus within a one to two month timeframe. An example includes the following incident:

Beginning in December 1991, a 35-year-old former student, who had graduated 6 years prior, carried out two sniper-style attacks on his old campus. On December 12, 1991, the subject fatally shot a janitor in an auditorium. Then on January 29, 1992, he shot and wounded a female graduate student as she waited in a building for her husband. It was during a third similar incident that the subject was killed by police. On February 10, 1992, the subject was shooting at a student housing complex near the campus. After a foot pursuit, the subject was killed by police. Though he had been rejected from the graduate program four years prior, the motive for the attacks was not clear.

See Appendix B for descriptions of the remaining two incidents.

---

[31] In two cases, the incidents were perpetrated by more than one subject so individual-level data regarding the subjects in those incidents were not gathered.

What were the subjects' affiliations with the IHEs?

In addition to basic descriptive information, the subjects' affiliations with the affected IHEs were examined. A subject's primary affiliation with the IHE was designated as either a *direct* affiliation (e.g., current or former student or employee) or *indirect* affiliation (e.g., a spouse, other immediate family member, non-spouse intimate partner, or friend of a current IHE student or employee). In addition, if the subject was affiliated with the affected IHE in more than one way, the subject's primary affiliation was captured (e.g., a full-time student who worked part-time on-campus was designated as a student rather than an employee).

Of those cases in which this information was reported ($n = 268$),[32] a majority of the subjects were identified as either current or former students at the affected IHE (60 percent, $n = 161$), while approximately one-tenth were current or former employees of the IHE (11 percent, $n = 29$). An additional 20 percent ($n = 53$) of the subjects were indirectly affiliated with the IHE through a personal relationship with a current IHE student and/or employee. In less than one-tenth of the cases (9 percent, $n = 25$), the subject had no known affiliation with the affected IHE. See Table 6 for additional information specific to each affiliation type.

Table 6: Characteristics and Casualties Listed by Subjects' IHE Affiliation

	Students ($n = 161$)	Employees ($n = 29$)	Indirectly Affiliated ($n = 53$)	No Known ($n = 25$)
Gender				
Male	93%	97%	96%	92%
Female	7%	3%	4%	8%
Average Age	25.5 ($n = 157$)	38.7 ($n = 27$)	29.9 ($n = 51$)	27.4 ($n = 23$)
Median	23	37	27	23
Mode	22	25[a]	19[b]	23
Range	17 to 62	18 to 62	18 to 55	16 to 51
Status				
Current	121	17	20	
Former	39	12	33	Not Applicable
Unknown	1	0	0	
Affiliation Details				
	Undergrad (62%) Graduate (18%) Alumni (8%) 2-year (6%) Voc/Technical (2%) Undetermined (5%)	Included range of positions, such as professors, librarians, security, janitorial, other.	60% ($n = 32$) current or former non-spouse intimate partners. 15% ($n = 8$) current or former spouses.	Not Applicable
Casualties (excluding subjects)				
Injuries	170	10	28	37
Deaths	193	27	37	22

[a] Multiple modes exist, smallest value is shown in Table 6 (25, 36, 37, 45).
[b] Multiple modes exist, smallest value is shown in Table 6 (19, 24).

---

[32] Multiple subject cases and those involving subjects whose affiliation could not be determined were excluded resulting in a total n of 268.

What method of attack was used?

Firearms were used most often (54 percent, $n = 148$), followed by knives/bladed weapons (21 percent, $n = 57$), a combination of weapons/methods (10 percent, $n = 26$), and strangulation either manually or with an implement (5 percent, $n = 14$). Of those incidents in which a combination of methods was used, most targets were strangled and stabbed. The remaining 27 incidents (10 percent) involved a blunt object, firebomb/incendiary/arson, explosives, poison, a vehicle, or a physical assault without a weapon.

Whom did the subjects harm?

Across all 272 incidents, the subjects caused 281 deaths and injured 247 individuals. Of the deaths, at least 190 were students and at least 72 were employees. Of the injured, at least 144 were students and at least 35 were employees. Not included in these numbers are the subjects themselves who were injured or killed either during or following the incident. In 26 percent ($n = 71$) of the incidents, the subject died of a self-inflicted injury incurred during implementation of the assault or within hours or days of the incident. In 4 percent of the incidents ($n = 11$), the subject survived his self-inflicted injuries and in an additional 4 percent of the incidents ($n = 10$), the subject was killed by law enforcement during or immediately following the assault.

QUALITATIVE OBSERVATIONS

Key elements of a thorough threat assessment include such items as the subject's motive and goal in carrying out an attack, triggering life events, target selection, and/or prior concerning or threatening behavior. These elements are at times difficult to discern due to the availability of information and subjectivity of their interpretation. Information related to these elements is particularly difficult to gather from open-sources, which do not always contain complete and accurate reporting.

Efforts were made to gather as much information as possible to provide an initial description of the motives and triggers, targeting, and pre-incident behaviors of concern. When the information was reported, judgments were made as to its completeness and apparent accuracy. A more in-depth analysis of each of these elements would require additional data other than what is available through open-source.

What factors motivated or triggered the attacks?

Generally, several categories were observed among the incidents regarding the factors that may have played a role in the subjects' decision to carry out the directed assault. These factors fall broadly within areas related to personal relations, academic performance, workplace issues, and/or individual stressors (see Table 7; for definitions, see Appendix C). Although it was recognized that multiple factors may have motivated or triggered the offenders' violent acts, efforts were made to identify the most prominent ones and the incidents were categorized accordingly. In 17 percent ($n = 45$) of the cases, either the motivating and/or triggering factors were completely unknown or they were less apparent as various factors specific to the subject and his/her environment appeared to influence the decision to engage in the violent behavior. Those incidents in which the motive and/or trigger was not apparent were excluded from Table 7.

Table 7: Factors that Motivated or Triggered the Directed Assaults

Categories	$n =$	%
Related to an Intimate Relationship	77	33.9
Retaliation for Specific Action(s)	31	13.7
Refused Advances or Obsession with the Target	23	10.1
Response to Academic Stress/Failure	23	10.1
Acquaintance/Stranger Based Sexual Violence	22	9.7
Psychotic Actions	18	7.9
Workplace Dismissal/Sanction	14	6.2
Need to Kill / Specific Victimology	7	3.1
Draw Attention to Self/Issue(s)	7	3.1
Bias Related	5	2.2
Total	227	100

As noted in Table 7, the most prevalent category identified related to current or former personal relationships between the subject and victim, followed by retaliation for specific actions. Future research should examine primary source materials, which may offer more insight into the underlying motives and triggers related to these incidents.

How did target selection compare with the actual victims?

Regarding the subject's apparent targeting and scope of his or her victims, efforts were made to distinguish those subjects who had specific targets from those who did not, and then designate whether the actual victims who were injured or killed appeared to be the intended victims. Various items were taken into account when determining targeting, including the subject, the setting in which the subject was functioning, the context of the situation with which he or she was faced (e.g., relationship breakup, academic or work suspension, imminent or actual academic failure, loss of job, or delusions), and the subject's relationship to the target (e.g., current or former intimate partner, co-worker, professor, classmate, stranger). Additionally, consideration was given to the subject's reported actions before, during, and after the attack. Specific examples of factors considered in the decision-making process include the following:

- indications of planning,
- method and manner of the attack,
- travel by the subject to a locale where a specific person's presence could reasonably be anticipated,
- apparent triggering event,
- admissions of intent or other communications by the subject reported before, during, and/or after the incident, and
- the nature of the subject's relationship with the victim(s) prior to the attack.

Targeting: Specifically Named Individuals

In nearly three-quarters of the incidents (73 percent, $n = 198$), subjects targeted one or more specifically named individuals. From context, their target selections appeared closely related to triggering events (e.g., romantic breakup, an academic or workplace failure, or a dispute), and, more often than not, were limited to the person or persons whom the subject may have blamed for causing the event. In a small fraction of these cases (2 percent, $n = 6$), there was also some indication that the subjects intended to harm one or more random persons beyond the individuals they blamed. An example of the latter situation includes the following incident:

> *On April 17, 1981, upset over failing grades and a possible second academic dismissal from the IHE, a 22-year-old student tossed a firebomb into the hallway of a dormitory and opened fire with a sawed-off shotgun as the occupants evacuated. Two students were killed. When police searched the subject's room, they found a gas mask, a second gun, and more than 100 shotgun shells as well as a notepad containing the name of one of the victims in the case. According to reports, this led police to believe that among the subject's random targets, there was at least one specific target whom the subject intended to harm.*

In over three-quarters of the incidents where specific individuals were targeted, these individuals were the only ones harmed (79 percent, $n = 156$). In the remaining cases ($n = 42$), the casualties included collateral victims[33] and/or victims of opportunity.[34] Examples of variations among these types of cases include:

Specific Individual Targeted and Additional Collateral Victim Harmed During the Incident:

On April 5, 1975, upset over failing his oral exam, a 25-year-old doctoral candidate shot and wounded an assistant professor from the review committee. The victim was sitting in a classroom with others who were waiting for a lecture to begin. Also wounded was a student bystander who came into the line of fire when he stood at the same time as the intended target. Reportedly, the subject had threatened the professor two days prior and a pistol was taken from him by campus police; however, he was not taken into custody at that time.

Specific Individual Targeted and Victim of Opportunity Killed During the Incident:

On December 17, 1983, at 11:30 p.m. on Saturday night, a 26-year-old subject who was not affiliated with the affected IHE, arrived at a dormitory to see his former girlfriend, a student, with whom he had become obsessed. When he arrived at her room, she reluctantly agreed to see him. When it became tense, the subject held the girlfriend, her roommate, and five others hostage using a silenced rifle. After the former girlfriend convinced him to release all but herself and her roommate, the subject fatally shot them both. He then drove off and shot himself in the head, but survived the wound.

Targeting: Random Individuals

In approximately one-fifth of the incidents (21 percent, *n* = 58), the subject's targeting appeared to be directed toward a single random individual or multiple random individuals. Examples of this type of targeting include the following:

Random Individual Targeted:

On May 17, 2001, a 55-year-old subject who was not affiliated with the affected IHE, fatally shot an assistant music professor on a walkway outside a dormitory. He then took his own life. According to a note left behind, the subject chose the victim at random. He had become obsessed with another professor on that campus whom he had dated briefly in 1966. Though he had had no contact with her for nearly three decades, in 1995 he began stalking her. Frustrated at being rebuffed, he decided to kill himself and take someone else with him. He hoped that person would be someone known to her. In the note he left, the subject wrote, "I considered multiple murder but realized it's pointless. I finally decided to murder just one person. Just one is sufficient to teach a lesson."

Multiple Random Individuals Targeted:

On September 26, 1977, distraught over pressures to perform from his parents, a 22-year-old student fatally shot his apartment manager, then grabbed a rifle and one of his handguns and went to the campus. He entered a typing lab in the Business Administration Building, then, in front of 30-40 students, fired off a few shots. One shot struck a teacher's aide. He then sought one of the fleeing

---

[33] "Collateral Victim" is defined as a person who was injured or killed during the execution of the attack and (a) was not specifically selected or contemplated in advance, and (b) whose actual harm was incidental during the execution of the attack.
[34] "Victim of Opportunity" is defined as a person who was injured or killed during the execution of the attack and (a) was not specifically selected or contemplated in advance, but (b) whose selection as an appropriate object of harm, consistent with the subject's apparent motive or goals, was made at the time of the incident.

What pre-incident behaviors were directed toward the targets?

Though information on the subjects' behaviors prior to the incidents was not always reported,
efforts were made to identify whether the subjects engaged in verbal and/or written threats,
stalking or harassing behaviors, and/or physically aggressive acts directed toward the targets
prior to the incidents. In 29 percent ($n = 79$) of the incidents, subjects engaged in one or more of
these actions directed toward the target. Figure 4 illustrates how these behaviors overlapped.

Figure 4

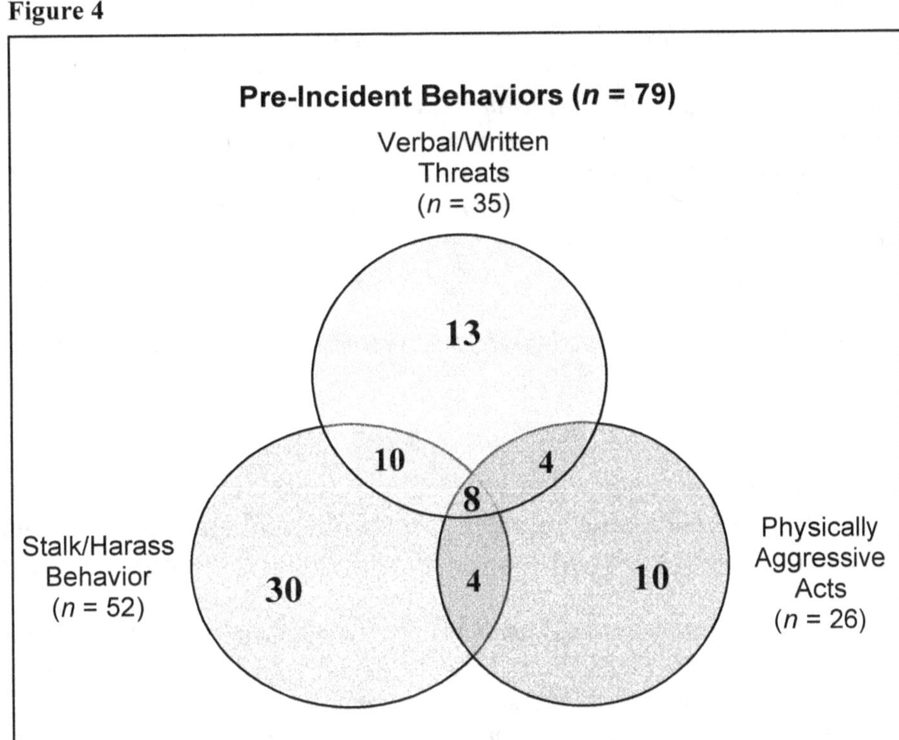

Verbal/Written Threats

In 35 incidents (13 percent), open-sources reported that the subjects made verbal and/or written
threats to cause harm to the target. These threats were both veiled and direct, and were conveyed
to the target or to a third party about the target. An example includes:

Stalking/Harassment

Open-sources reported stalking or harassing behavior in 52 incidents (19 percent). These behaviors occurred within the context of a current or former romantic relationship or in academic and other non-romantic settings. They took on various forms, including written communications (conventional and electronic), telephonic contact, and harassment of the target and/or the target's friends/family. Subjects also followed, visited, or damaged property belonging to target(s) or their families prior to the attack. Examples include the following incidents:

On July 25, 1989, a 24-year-old subject who was not affiliated with the affected IHE, tracked down his former girlfriend who had moved to another state to avoid him, and confronted her in the IHE parking lot as she walked with a male friend. When she would not go with the subject, he shot and killed them both. The subject had hired a private detective agency to track her down and was able to obtain information on the victim through bank records and the IHE registrar.

On April 10, 1996, upset over losing his friendship with the victim, a 19-year-old student confronted his former friend on campus, fatally shot him in the back of the head, flipped him over with his foot and fired another shot into his chest. Months prior to the incident, the victim reported to IHE administrators that the subject had been harassing him by sending e-mails and calling numerous times. The subject, who had completed his degree requirements in December 1995, was told by administrators to stay away from the campus. On the day of the incident, in accordance with an agreement he made with the IHE, the subject had informed the dean of his intended presence on campus that day. The subject had completed his degree requirements and was awaiting graduation.

Physically Aggressive Acts

Open-sources reported that subjects engaged in physically aggressive acts toward the targets in 26 incidents (10 percent). These behaviors took the form of physical assaults, menacing actions with weapons, or repeated physical violence to intimate partners. An example includes:

On August 12, 1996, upset over his girlfriend (student) breaking up with him 10 days prior, a 27-year-old subject (not affiliated with the IHE) arranged to meet her on campus. Once there, he fatally shot her in the parking lot, then himself. Witnesses described that the subject had been physically and mentally abusive toward the victim during their one-year relationship. Just four months before this attack, the subject held a 13-inch blade to the victim's throat, tying her hands with a scarf, and threatening to kill her.

Did others observe concerning behaviors just prior to the incidents?

Information on whether the subjects engaged in concerning pre-incident behaviors was not always reported. Open-sources may report their presence, but rarely confirm their absence. With this in mind, attempts were made to explore any discernable behaviors that may have occurred just prior to the incidents and warranted concern by those surrounding the subjects. The behaviors noted are purely descriptive and should not be considered comparative or predictive.

Concerning behaviors were observed by friends, family, associates, professors, or law enforcement in 85 incidents (31 percent).[35] These behaviors included, but were not limited to: paranoid ideas, delusional statements, changes in personality or performance, disciplinary problems on campus, depressed mood, suicidal ideation, non-specific threats of violence, increased isolation, "odd" or "bizarre" behavior, and interest in or acquisition of weapons. Examples include the following:

On May 19, 1936, possibly upset over academic pressures, a 19-year-old freshman fatally shot one student and wounded another as the students entered his dorm room. He then killed himself. He had reportedly purchased two guns from a mail order house a few days earlier. When this was discovered, the subject was ordered to turn the weapons over to the dean, which he promised a student adviser he would do. The subject's father also stated his son's recent letters had been "strange and hard to understand." A classmate stated that the subject had been "telling us fellows for a week that he had been planning suicide."

On January 26, 1992, a 22-year-old campus police officer pulled over a nursing student whom he did not know, drove her to a deserted campus parking lot, removed her clothing and shot her 14 times. Prior to the incident, the subject was linked to other crimes, which were known to the IHE. He was suspected in a series of campus fires, firing a bullet through a dormitory window, inventing a break-in, calling a suspect at home, and phoning in a bomb threat.

In 29 percent ($n = 25$) of the incidents involving concerning behaviors, the offenders also exhibited one or more acts involving stalking/harassment, written/verbal threats, or physically aggressive acts toward the target.

In those cases in which concerning behaviors were not observed ($n = 187$), media reports described other significant criminal, violent, or mental health histories unrelated to the incident ($n = 14$, 8 percent). This included multiple criminal or violent acts, a series of psychiatric hospitalizations, and/or the presence of psychotic symptoms over an extended period of time. An example is:

On January 12, 1980, the 24-year-old student manager of the tennis team fatally stabbed a campus tennis star outside of the dorm. During trial it was revealed that the subject had been expelled from six schools due to behavior problems, saw at least a dozen mental health professionals, and spent time in at least six hospitals. In addition, witnesses described specific violent incidents, such as hitting a neighbor's son with a hammer, setting fire to his house, attacking a stranger on a train platform, and striking a co-worker over the head with a metal pipe.

---

[35] It should be noted that those persons who reported the concerning behaviors were not necessarily trained in the recognition of psychiatric or psychological symptoms.

CONSIDERATIONS

Campus threat assessment teams that seek to employ reasoned and effective risk mitigation strategies may recognize the potential significance of findings presented in this preliminary report.[36]

General Observations

Several general observations concerning the data have relevance to the domain of threat assessment and threat management.

- Incidents of targeted violence are a year-round issue. Campus safety resources may be required throughout the calendar year, not just during the academic year.

- On-campus targeted violence is not the only challenge, as 20 percent of the incidents took place off-campus or in non-campus IHE locations against targeted IHE members. This suggests that communication between campus safety professionals and municipal law enforcement agencies is essential.

- Of those incidents that occurred at on-campus or non-campus sites ($n = 217$), 36 percent took place in administrative/academic/services buildings, 28 percent took place in residential buildings, and 27 percent took place in parking lots or campus grounds. On-campus mitigation plans should equally cover responses to IHE buildings, IHE operated residences, and IHE parking lots and grounds.

- Only 3 percent of on/non-campus attackers ($n = 217$) moved *between* buildings. Of those that were carried out *within* the same building ($n = 159$), only 4 percent of the attackers moved to different locales (e.g., classrooms, offices, hallways). Though much attention has been given to the phenomenon of the "traveling" attacker, in context, it actually is a rare event. This finding may have tactical and strategic ramifications for first responders and emergency management professionals.

- Firearms and knives/bladed weapons were used most frequently (75 percent) during the incidents. The remaining 25 percent of the incidents involved strangulation, blunt objects, poison, vehicles, explosives, incendiary/arson methods, or physical assaults without a weapon. Understanding the varied weapons used in these incidents may prompt investigators to look beyond whether a subject possesses or has access to a more traditional weapon (firearm or knife) when evaluating his or her risk.

---

[36] Before implementing a threat assessment model, IHEs should consult with legal counsel as they develop their threat assessment process, policies, and protocols. Specifically, legal counsel should be asked to review and consider relevant federal and state statutes about information sharing, e.g., the *Family Education Rights and Privacy Act* (*FERPA*), as well as those concerning an IHE's civil rights obligations (e.g., the *Civil Rights Act of 1964* and the *Rehabilitation Act of 1973*). More information can be found at: http://www2.ed.gov/about/offices/list/ocr/index.html.

Diversity of the Subject Population

A great deal of concern is given to conducting threat assessments of current students who may pose a threat of targeted violence. This level of concern is not entirely misplaced as current students represented 45 percent ($n = 121$) of the subjects in those incidents in which the subjects' affiliations were identified ($n = 268$). The violence documented in the remaining 55 percent of the cases included former students (15 percent), current and former employees (11 percent), subjects indirectly affiliated with the IHE (20 percent), and subjects with no known affiliation with the IHE (9 percent). The unique and open nature of most universities necessitates acknowledgement of the many diverse threats to campus safety. It is clear that focusing solely on the student attacker as a potential threat to campus safety ignores the fact that many IHEs are workplaces, residences, and communities that routinely host a wide range of activities that attract a variety of individuals, many of whom do not have any direct relationship to the college or university.

From a threat assessment perspective, the fact that 30 percent of the subjects were either unaffiliated or indirectly affiliated with the IHE through students or employees, three-quarters of whom were current or former spouses or intimate partners, challenges campus and law enforcement personnel to design a threat assessment capability that can also identify and assess threats that go beyond their student and employee populations. By establishing connections to community resources ahead of time, campus safety professionals may enhance their ability to prevent a threat from materializing that originated from an indirectly affiliated subject.

Additionally, although the average subject age was 28 ($n = 260$, *Mdn* = 25, mode=20), these preliminary findings highlight the wide range of offenders' ages (16 to 62) and suggest the need for a flexible analysis and response protocol. As developmental issues and situational stressors change across a lifespan, standard practices should incorporate multidimensional risk factors germane to specific stages, from adolescence to mature adulthood. Similarly, IHEs traditionally host multi-ethnic, culturally diverse populations, further requiring contextually appropriate considerations. While this phase of the project did not address the ethnic backgrounds of the subjects, it is anticipated that the Department of Education and the FBI, in the next stages of this research, will highlight the need for IHE threat assessment teams to recognize and assess behaviors exhibited by a pool of individuals representing a broad range of ages, cultures, past life experiences, and current situational contexts.

Diversity of Criminal and Other Concerning Behaviors

IHE campuses essentially function as mini-societies that must deal with the same types of societal issues found in almost any city or town in the United States. Whether the setting is a more traditional campus with distinct boundaries, an urban campus that is interlaced within a larger community, or somewhere in between, most campuses must contend with their own social norms, economy and culture. IHEs must then establish an infrastructure capable of providing the necessary services, support and protection to students, staff, and others who may have contact with the IHE. Looking at the protection side alone, as a mini-society, IHEs must contend with the full range of crimes committed by or against its members.

All forms of targeted violence were found among the incidents. The identified incidents dealt with domestic violence, workplace violence, stalking and obsessions, sexual assaults resulting in homicide, individualistic stressors, subjects acting on delusional beliefs, as well as serial killers. Because of this diversity of crime, those responsible for threat assessment may need to build a program that is flexible and comprehensive enough to address all aspects of targeted violence. This may require university threat assessment teams to employ a wider breadth of resources that will educate and support them as they address the full range of targeted violence.

CONCLUSION

For this paper, researchers relied on open-source information to capture the nature and magnitude of violence affecting America's colleges and universities. Therefore, the observations and recommendations are necessarily limited, and readers should be cautious to avoid drawing broad-based conclusions. What is offered here, then, is not the end of the process, but a preliminary look at the scope of this issue. Several of the key elements explored included the attackers' intent with regard to target selection, interpersonal relationships, personal stressors, and triggering events. Each of these elements seemingly played a significant role in the offenders' decision to commit an act of violence. In nearly three-quarters of the captured incidents, the offender appeared to have targeted one or more specifically named individuals. Only in a small percentage of the cases was there some indication that random persons were also targeted along with specific individuals. Hence, understanding what leads an offender to exclusively target random individuals remains a complex and difficult challenge.

For years, colleges and universities have worked to address this challenge—to create safe campuses where academic and personal growth can flourish. In the wake of the Virginia Tech tragedy, many universities were confronted with the troubling reality that one person can, in a few brief moments, devastate a college community through an act of targeted violence. In the effort to thwart such individuals, IHEs have created threat assessment teams. These teams typically comprise representatives from various departments within the college or university, including academic affairs, student affairs, the IHE's general legal counsel, mental health services, and public safety. IHE threat assessment teams seek to thoroughly evaluate persons of concern who may pose a potential risk of violence and generally engage in a three-step process:

- Identify individuals, whose behavior causes concern or disruption on or off campus, affecting IHE members such as students, faculty, or other staff.

- Assess whether the identified individual possesses the intent and ability to carry out an attack against the IHE or members of the IHE community, and if the individual has taken any steps to prepare for the attack.

- Manage the threat posed by the individual, to include disrupting potential plans of attack, mitigating the risk, and implementing strategies to facilitate long-term resolution.

IHE threat assessment teams that perform this important function are routinely faced with several key issues during each evaluation: identifying the specific behaviors that are suggestive of an attack against persons affiliated with an IHE (including students, faculty, and staff); considering whether concerning, suicidal, or threatening behaviors are warning signs of a violent act; and fostering a secure environment while simultaneously promoting academic freedom and creative expression, and protecting student privacy.[37]

---

[37] The threat assessment process is based on the premise that each situation should be viewed and assessed individually and guided by the facts. Judgments about an individual's risk of violence should be based upon an analysis of his/her behaviors and the context in which they occur. Blanket characterizations, demographic profiles, or stereotypes do not provide a reliable basis for making judgments of the threat posed by a particular individual.

With these challenges in mind, the participating agencies in this study have collaborated in an effort to further understand targeted violence at colleges and universities. The goal of this phase of research was to identify and examine incidents of targeted violence that have occurred at IHEs or against members of the IHE community. As the project enters into the next phase, the FBI and the Department of Education will thoroughly examine case files and investigative records from campus attacks in an effort to better serve the professionals who work to ensure campus safety. The next phase will include a more detailed examination of characteristics that were difficult or impossible to measure due to inadequate or missing information in the open-sources (e.g., mental illness, past behavior). The researchers are optimistic that by exploring violence against IHE students, faculty, and staff, some offenders can be identified prior to an attack and many lives can be saved.

APPENDIX A: IHE Definitions

IHE Campus/Facility: IHE grounds (e.g., areas between buildings, landscaped areas), parking lots, buildings (e.g., classroom buildings, dining halls, student unions, research centers, dormitories, fraternity/sorority houses, other university-sponsored student housing), and built venues (e.g., stadiums) that are owned, leased, operated, or reserved by the IHE for permanent or temporary use.

IHE Employee: Member of an IHE's faculty, staff (e.g., mental health counselors, building maintenance personnel, campus law enforcement, financial aid counselors, medical personnel), or administration (e.g., dean, president, provost, vice president), an IHE contractor, or an individual employed by an IHE contractor.

IHE Event: IHE sporting, ceremonial (e.g., graduation, award dinners), entertainment, and educational activities (e.g., student government meetings) sponsored or sanctioned by the IHE or an association affiliated with the IHE.

IHE Student: Individual enrolled in a college or university (e.g., undergraduate, graduate, full- and part-time). The student may still be enrolled at the IHE even though he or she is not registered for classes at the time of the incident.

Non-Campus: "Any building or property owned or controlled by a student organization that is officially recognized by the institution; or Any building or property owned or controlled by an institution that is used in direct support of, or in relation to, the institution's educational purposes, is frequently used by students, and is not within the same reasonably contiguous geographic area of the institution."[38] Examples include research facilities, university-owned hospitals, off-campus student housing facility owned by a third party that has a written contract with the institution to provide student housing, student residential facility owned or controlled by the institution, a publicly owned athletic stadium that is leased by the institution for its football games.

Off-Campus: All other buildings or facilities that may be used by IHE students or IHE employees for housing and/or recreation but are not officially associated with an IHE. Examples include privately leased apartments, privately owned residences, social clubs, or restaurants.

On-Campus: "Any building or property owned or controlled by an institution within the same reasonably contiguous geographic area and used by the institution in direct support of, or in a manner related to, the institution's educational purposes, including residence halls."[39] Sorority or fraternity houses that are located within the same reasonably contiguous geographic area of the institution are included as on-campus, even if they are not controlled or owned by the IHE.

---

[38] *Higher Education Act*, 34 C.F.R. 668.46(a).
[39] *Ibid.*

APPENDIX B: Additional Examples of Incidents

Subjects who moved from one location/building to another:

On August 12, 1986, a 29-year-old student went on a shooting rampage on campus, injuring four and fatally shooting one. The subject had purchased two guns out of state the day before. When he returned, he went straight to the campus laboratory where he fatally shot one of his intended targets, a lab technician with whom he had worked. He then ran to the campus financial aid office in a second building, where he shot and wounded three more people, including the financial aid director who was another intended target. After firing shots at campus officers behind the second building, he raced into a third building, where he shot and wounded a security officer. After being cornered on a stairwell, he eventually surrendered to police. The attack appeared to be related to a dispute over $717 in financial aid. He reportedly was due to receive the funds beginning the next month.

On November 1, 1991, a 28-year-old former student opened fire in two different buildings on campus. The subject had received his doctoral degree the previous May. Months before the shooting, he wrote five letters explaining the reasons for his planned actions. Intended for news organizations, they stated that he was angry and jealous that his doctoral dissertation had not received a prestigious academic award and he was upset over perceived mistreatment and his inability to find work. The subject allegedly had specific targets that included his academic advisor, the chairman of his department, an assistant professor and his former roommate. After fatally shooting them in his department building, he then walked three blocks to another building and asked to see the assistant vice president for academic affairs. After fatally shooting her, he turned and wounded the student assistant seated there. He eventually fatally shot himself.

On March 24, 1999, a 25-year-old former student fired a gun in the Agricultural Building on campus, striking a door. The shot just missed two female students in the hallway by a few inches. Approximately 20 minutes later, the subject fired another shot at a student sitting in a courtyard on the same campus, striking the student in the left arm. Though media reports did not reveal a motive for the attacks, they did connect him to another shooting on another campus the following day. In that incident, the subject fired a shot in the hallway of a new academic building on a campus with which he had no known affiliation. The shot grazed the side of a female who was on campus visiting her father, a professor on that campus.

Subjects who moved between multiple locales within the same building:

On April 25, 1950, a 54-year-old professor went to the second floor office of the college president, fatally shooting him. He then went downstairs to the office department chair, the subject's immediate supervisor, and fatally shot him. The subject then returned home and killed himself. Investigators found the body and several notes. Reportedly, the subject suspected he would be fired but had not been officially informed. When the new college catalogue was issued on the morning of the incident, the subject saw that his name was not included after 24 years with the college.

On November 11, 1971, a 21-year-old non-affiliated subject entered a campus church with a rifle, pick ax, and a sledgehammer. When he encountered the caretaker, the subject fatally shot him in the back. He then used the sledgehammer to smash statues, pews, and windows. He then ran outside, randomly firing at passersby, injuring four. He was later killed by police at the scene. Following the shooting, the subject's father blamed LSD, stating that his son had become a religious fanatic, convinced that "Christ was an imposter."

On October 6, 1979, shortly after midnight, a 19-year-old student opened fire at a crowded fraternity party in a dorm, shooting five students. He then ran outside and shot two more students. In total, five students were injured, two were killed. His defense attorney blamed a "second personality" and brain damage from a car wreck as a child. The prosecutors stated that the subject had attended one of the fraternity's parties two weeks prior and was mad that his two-dollar cover charge was not refunded after police broke it up.

On May 4, 1983, a former employee (age not reported) entered a campus library, shot and wounded the director of libraries in his office. He then walked into an adjacent conference room with 20 people inside and fired two shots at his former supervisor, missing both times. After reloading his weapon in a restroom, he left the floor and headed to the main desk. Once there, he unloaded his weapon, put it down and waited for police. The subject had been fired from the library just three months prior after 19 years of service.

On January 16, 2002, a 43-year-old former student went to the offices of the college dean and a professor, fatally shooting them both. He then descended a stairway into a common area and opened fire on a crowd of students, killing one and wounding three others. Days before the shooting, faculty had informed the subject that they were dismissing him from the school due to his failing grades. Police said the shooting occurred after he arrived to protest his dismissal.

On May 9, 2003, at 4 p.m., a 62-year-old former student, who had also been employed by the IHE in the past, opened fire on the exterior of the business school building on campus. He then used a sledgehammer to smash his way through the entry. He reportedly fired hundreds of rounds of ammunition while he wandered the halls of the building. One student was fatally shot, while a professor and student were wounded. The subject was reportedly looking for a computer lab technician whom the subject had sued for hacking into his Web site and he wanted to punish the university for protecting him. The attack ended about 11 p.m. when officers shot and wounded the subject.

Subjects who carried out multiple attacks on the same campus within 1-2 months:

Starting in February 1982, four separate shootings took place on a college campus and were committed by a 32-year-old former student, later identified as a neo-Nazi serial killer. On February 1, the subject fatally shot a popular local pastor in a men's room in a classroom building on campus. Later, on August 9 and August 27, he shot at two employees also in restrooms located on campus, missing one and killing the other. Three days later, he fatally shot a 17-year-old student enrolled in a high school equivalency program at a bus stop in front of the campus. The subject was also connected to another sniper-style attack that took place off-campus at a train station that June. The victim wounded in that attack was not affiliated with the affected IHE.

On August 31 and September 22, 1999, a 41-year-old unemployed funeral embalmer and father of two set off two pipe bombs in restrooms in administrative and classroom buildings on campus. Both explosions were accompanied within minutes by racist phone calls to a local TV station, and the last one included a warning that the two blasts were "just the beginning." Though there was only minimal damage with no injuries, 400 students withdrew from the university in the aftermath. The subject was a former vending company employee who once had a delivery route at the campus and had serviced machines in the two buildings where the bombs were detonated. He also held a university-issued ID card for this job, and a former coworker told investigators he did not return it when he left the company in July 1999.

Examples of stalking or harassing behaviors exhibited by subjects prior to the incidents:

Acquaintance Harassment:
On November 29, 1992, a box of candy was received by a 26-year-old female student. The student did not eat the candy; rather, she turned it over to police. According to the authorities, the candy was spiked with thallium. The unmarked package was traced to a former student who had studied at the IHE from August 1990 to May 1991. The target had rejected the subject's romantic advances and leveled verified charges of harassment against him, causing him to be removed from the IHE. The subject had sent a similar package to another female student in another state. In that case, the victim consumed the candy as did her roommates. The victim and three others were hospitalized. After the subject was identified, it was revealed that he had a history of stalking the second victim in their native country of Belgium.

Stranger-Based Stalking:
On January 13, 1998, a 27-year-old subject, not affiliated with the affected IHE, killed an IHE campus police officer after striking him more than 20 times with a hatchet. The officer had been sitting in his squad car doing paperwork at the time. Witnesses would later testify that the subject stalked the victim prior to the incident and repeatedly informed family and friends that he wanted to kill a cop.

Academic-Based Harassment:
On August 24, 2006, upset over his dismissal from a master's degree program, a 25-year-old former graduate student set four small fires at a professor's home. The professor and his two teenage children escaped the home without injury and the fires were extinguished with minimal damage to the home. The subject was later captured in a wooded area nearby where he had tried to kill himself with a drug overdose. In October 2005, the victim had filed a complaint with the police department that the subject was making harassing phone calls to his home. Additionally, the subject had sent e-mails to his internship supervisor that were sufficiently "aggressive" in tone that a police officer was stationed outside her classroom for the last three classes the subject attended.

APPENDIX C: Definitions of Incident Categories

Acquaintance/Stranger-Based Sexual Violence—Directed assaults that included sexual violence between persons known or not known to each other, excluding those subjects and targets who were current or former intimates.

Bias Related—Directed assaults in which the subject appeared to be motivated by a bias against the target based on race/ethnicity, religion, or other characteristics.

Draw Attention to Self/Issue(s) —Directed assaults in which the subject's actions were intended to draw attention to the subject, the subject's actions, or a specific issue other than one based on bias.

Need to Kill/Specific Victimology—Directed assaults in which the subject appears to be motivated by a general need to kill or selection of a target that matches a victim profile (a set of demographic or other perceived static traits that the subject(s) sought in selecting a target).

Psychotic Actions[40]—Directed assaults where the subject's actions appeared to be as a result of delusions, paranoia or hallucinations.

Refused Advances or Obsession with the Target—Directed assaults in which the subject's actions appeared to be a response to romantic or interpersonal rejection and there was no clear indication that the subject and the target had an intimate relationship. This also includes a subject who was obsessed with a target, of which the target was never aware.

Related to an Intimate Relationship—Directed assaults in which the subject retaliated against a current or former intimate partner (e.g., husband, wife, boyfriend, girlfriend) for any reason (e.g., breakup, divorce, affair, filing court papers). This could also include retaliation against a proxy for that intimate partner (e.g., the current partner, or mistress).

Response to Academic Stress/Failure—Directed assaults in which the subject's actions appeared to be the products of academic stress, rejection or failure.

Retaliation for Specific Action(s) —Directed assaults in which the subject's actions were in retaliation for a specific act (including statements) committed by or perceived to be committed by the target, but that does not meet the definition of the other options. The retaliatory attack could be directed toward a third party.

Undetermined—Open-source did not contain enough information to determine one clear motive or trigger for these incidents.

Workplace Dismissal/Sanction—Directed assaults in which the subject appeared to be responding to an impending or actual dismissal/suspension or forced resignation, or was retaliating for a past or present workplace legal action or other difficulty.

---

[40] For a discussion on "psychotic action" see Junginger, J. (1996). Psychosis and Violence: The Case for a Content Analysis of Psychotic Experience. *Schizophrenia Bulletin,* 22 (1), 91-103.